THE BASIS

OF

THE THEOSOPHICAL SOCIETY

BY

ANNIE BESANT

President of the Theosophical Society

THE BASIS

OF

THE THEOSOPHICAL SOCIETY

BY

ANNIE BESANT

President of the Theosophical Society

WILDSIDE PRESS

The Basis of the Theosophical Society

Originally published in the *Theosophist*
for February, 1907, in order that the
Theosophical Society might know, before
proceeding to election, the views of the
nominee for the Presidency.

THE BASIS OF THE THEOSOPHICAL SOCIETY [1]

RECENT events have caused much discussion and many searchings of heart as regards the true basis of the Theosophical Society, and it is clear that there is a division of opinion among the thoughtful members; this division is natural, for there is much to be said on the question: "Should a nucleus of Universal Brotherhood be, or not be, all-inclusive?" It may be well that members should consider what is to be said on each side, and that each should make up his mind as to the ground he occupies. Those who, on either side, airily dismiss the matter as though their own view were indisputably true, and the only one which any rational person can hold, show more prejudice than wisdom. To this question the words of the Lord Buddha may be said to apply: "You did right to doubt, for it was a doubtful matter."

[1] Published in the *Theosophist* for February, 1907, in order that the Theosophical Society might know, before proceeding to election, the views of the nominee for the Presidency.

The one side starts with the statement: " This is a Universal Brotherhood and is founded on a spiritual unity; Spirit is inclusive, all-embracing, and a Universal Brotherhood founded on the Spirit can exclude none; hence no one should be expelled from the Theosophical Society." This argument appeals to a very large number of people, and it has a convincing ring about it. But is it as convincing as it sounds? Is it not founded on an error? The Theosophical Society is not a ¡Universal Brotherhood, but a nucleus thereof, and a nucleus and its cell are not co-extensive. The Universal Brotherhood of humanity is not made by the Theosophical Society; a man does not enter it when he becomes a member of the Theosophical Society, nor leave it when he ceases to be a Theosophical member. The Universal Brotherhood is a fact in nature, beyond our creating or our destroying; the purest saint and the vilest criminal are brothers in fact, in truth. Nor would there be any sense or object in making a 'Society' which should be co-extensive with humanity. The mere fact that the Society has objects, of which the applicant for membership must approve, differentiates it from humanity at large and makes a limitation. A man who denies Universal Brotherhood cannot be a member of the Theosophical Society, but he is, and must ever remain, a human

brother. It is, then, not the fact of Brotherhood but the recognition of it which entitles a
man to membership in the Theosophical Society
to become part of the ' nucleus,' and a further
guarantee demanded from two members, that the
candidate is a "fit and proper person to become
a member of the Theosophical Society," implies
that the recognition is believed to be not merely a lip but also a life-recognition. If these
facts are so—and that they are so is surely
undeniable—it follows that a member may be
expelled if he ceases to be "a fit and proper
person" to be part of the nucleus; conditions
of admission imply the corresponding right to
exclude, when the conditions cease to exist.
Admission and exclusion are correlatives; one
who is admitted may be excluded. The fact
that a man cannot be excluded from the Universal Brotherhood of humanity goes with the fact
that he cannot be admitted into it. Hence the
fundamental statement put forward by those who
deny all right of exclusion from the Theosophical
Society is founded on a confusion of thought, a
false identification of a Society which is a nucleus with the Universal Brotherhood within which
it lives.

It may be urged that, while this is so, it
would be better for the Society to have a different basis, and to abandon the power of expul-

sion. That is arguable, though it is difficult to see how such a Society could formulate its conditions of membership; it would seem that it could have no conditions and no definite membership. However that may be, such a Society would have a different basis from the actual Theosophical Society, and we are concerned with the Society as it is. Those who wish to have a Society on a different basis are surely at liberty to form one, but it should be understood that it would be a new Society.

The next question is: "What constitutes fitness and propriety for membership in the nucleus called the Theosophical Society?" A nucleus is a centre of vital forces, a centre from which they radiate, causing organisation and growth in the surrounding body. Through this particular nucleus play forces which spiritualise humanity, and lead it towards the realisation of Universal Brotherhood; when that is realised by every one, the use of the affirmation of Universal Brotherhood will be over, and the Society as a nucleus in that Brotherhood will cease to be; if it is to continue to live, it will have to be reincarnated with new objects.

The first, and perhaps we may find the only fitness and propriety necessary to membership, is a recognition of the Truth of Brotherhood, the wish to help it to emerge from latency into activity. The desire to help in bringing about the general realisation of Universal Brotherhood is the primary fitness and propriety which are sought. This makes a man a vehicle through which can work the forces that make for the realisation of Brotherhood. The Love-force in him makes him one through which the Love-forces without him can play. And I think that this desire to help, evidenced by work which does help others towards the realisation of Brotherhood, is the only fitness and propriety that our Society can rightly demand.

I fully recognise and frankly confess that the acceptance of this view would occasionally keep among us members who would discredit the Society in the eyes of the ordinary man of the world, either by falling below the accepted morality of the time and place, or by rising so much above it as to be unintelligible, and therefore hated and suspected by the masses of average people. But I think that this temporary disadvantage is less than the introduction of the disintegrating forces of self-righteousness and contempt, which find their channels in the prosecution and expulsion of a member for a moral lapse. The presence in the Society of a man who falls below the accepted standard of morality in any respect can do little harm, when it is generally understood that the Society seeks to

raise the level of morality by right argument
and by the noble examples of its best members,
rather than by the infliction of penalties on its
worst. A man may do most evil things that
deserve and that meet with sternest condemnation,
and yet, having the root of the matter in him
in desire and effort to help, may remain a "fit
and proper person" to be a member of the
Theosophical Society. If penalty is to be inflicted
on wrong-doing, it is difficult to draw the line
between wrong-doing which is permissible and
wrong-doing which is not permissible in the
Society; if profligacy be penalised, at what level
of profligacy must the Society begin to exclude?
an occasional lapse from virtue? fairly constant
unclean living? "sowing wild oats" to the ruin
of many a wife and maiden? will it authorise
inquisition into the private lives of its members,
encourage secret accusations, or only punish those
who break the eleventh commandment: "Thou
shalt not be found out"?

A member may hold any theological opinion
he pleases: he cannot be excluded for teaching
everlasting torture, or the perpetual cremation of
miraculously-preserved unbaptised infants, or the
predestined damnation of souls presently to be
created, or the small number of the saved, or
the literal golden and bejewelled gates of the
New Jerusalem, or the physical immortality of

Mrs. Eddy or of Hiram Butler, etc., etc. All these matters are left to reason and argument, and no penalty may be inflicted on a Theosophist for his religious views, however bizarre or erroneous. It is rightly held that error is better combated by reason than by penalty, and although it may be said in a way that this policy of tolerance opens the door to every form of theological licentiousness, it is yet felt that this risk is a small one compared with the introduction of a principle, the legal end of which is the stake or the Inquisition. Our religious liberty of opinion—irreligious licence, say dogmatists—is secure.

But may we not have religious liberty and the enforcement of a common level of conduct, above which members may rise, but below which they may not sink? Shall we give liberty of opinion on moral as well as on religious questions? Here some members call a halt. They would not allow a member to hold opinions leading to murder, theft, adultery, any sexual irregularity, or other evil ways. Does the Theosophical Society enforce on its members a moral code, the transgression of which is punishable with expulsion? I do not consider that the Theosophical Society has any moral code binding on its members. That such a code does not exist in fact is clear, for no written or printed copy thereof can be produced.

Does it consist in a common consensus of opinions? though that would not be a code. If so, what are the opinions? Is polygamy moral or immoral? But many of our good members in the East are polygamists. Is polyandry moral or immoral? We have members who belong to a community where polyandry is practised. Is prostitution moral or immoral? I fear that the record of all our members is not quite clean on this point; shall they be expelled? On matters connected with the relation of the sexes some very great Initiates have taught most peculiar and, to our minds, outrageous doctrines in the past; should we expel Socrates, Plato, Moses, Vyāsa? We have no code; we hold up lofty ideals, inspiring examples, and we trust to these for the compelling power to lift our members to a high moral level, but we have no code with penalties for the infringement of its provisions.

Can we take the average social opinion of any place and time for a code? *e.g.*, in the West a polygamist should be expelled, and in the East should be regarded as fit and proper for membership? 'Public opinion' would then become our moral code. But would this be satisfactory? It means stagnation, not progress; it means death, not life. Such a principle would exclude from our ranks the greatest martyrs of the past, the pioneers of every race and time. Is the Theosophical Society to be of those who kill the prophets in every age, and build their tombs long afterwards when the age has risen to the level of the martyred prophets? While it is easy for every age to be sure that it only kills and persecutes evil men, posterity often reverses the verdict and apotheosises those whom its ancestors branded. Never a Jew, who, on the evening of the first Good Friday, congratulated himself and his friends for having purged Jewish Society by slaying a blasphemer, a deceiver of the people, and a stirrer-up of trouble, dreamed that a later Society would regard the martyred evil-doer as its Savior from evil. Such revenges has history, and wise men who study the lesson do not readily pick up the stones to slay.

Supposing a man oppose a triumphant majority, and seek to gather round him those who think like himself, thus undoubtedly causing 'agitation' and disturbance in a Branch or Section; what should be done with him? My answer would be: " Leave him alone for a time; if he force himself on Branch meetings, or behave in a way to make the Branch rooms unusable by the majority, then he may rightly be excluded from Branch premises, and compelled to carry on his agitation outside, but he should not be expelled

from the Society. At the most he might be
expelled from the Branch, wherein physical con-
tact is inevitable, and where one may disturb a
hundred. Every reform begins with a few, and,
if valuable, extends till it becomes a majority.
The workers against slavery in the United
States were regarded as pestilent agitators, were
tarred and feathered, and carried outside the
limits of the townships. Yet in the long run
those abused agitators abolished slavery. That
which a majority brands as 'causing agitation' a
minority regards as the defence of a great
principle. Time alone can judge, not the number
of the moment. Better a temporary inconvenience
than the violent stifling of opinion. If the
opinion be wrong, time will destroy it :
" Truth alone conquers, not falsehood. " If
it be right, time will crown it, and great
the reward of those who saw it in its uncrowned
days : " Let truth and falsehood grapple ; who
ever knew truth put to the worse in a fair
encounter ? "

H. P. B. warned us that the great danger of
the Society lay in its becoming a sect. Above
all things, therefore, should we guard liberty of
thought and speech, and most zealously of all,
when the thought and speech are antagonistic to
our own. Truth is pure gold ; it cannot be
burned up in the fire of discussion, only the

dross can be burned away. "The fire shall try every man's work, of what sort it is."

The outcome of this argument evidently re-iterates the view that the fitness and propriety of a man for membership in the Theosophical Society depend on his desire to help in bringing about the general realisation of Universal Brotherhood; and if this desire be questioned in any particular case on the ground that he teach-es wrong doctrines or wrong ways, and, there-fore, is hindering, not helping, then it would be cogent to enquire whether, as a matter of fact, he has helped any to realise Brotherhood, and the testimony that he has thus helped would be final.

I do not question the right of any Branch to exclude from its platform any person; it can choose as speakers on its platform such people only who voice the views of the majority on religion, philosophy, and ethics; this is within its right, whether its policy be wise or not. But it should not wish to exclude from all platforms of all Branches those with whom it disagrees.

I know that there are many in the Society, good people whom I respect, who will think that this article embodies a most dangerous doc-trine, and who will ask: "Should not we shut out polluting influences from our families? Should we not keep the nucleus pure, so

that spiritual life may play through it?"
To the first question I answer: "Yes; because
in the family there are children, who should be
guarded until strong enough to guard themselves;
but the Theosophical Society does not consist of
children, but of grown men and women, and it
does not need the shelter rightly given to the
young." To the second question I answer: "The
purer the nucleus the more will the spiritual
life pour through it, but is the nucleus rendered
pure by expelling one here and one there whom
we may manage to convict of some evil teaching or practice? We leave within it hundreds
who are guilty of other evils, and we cannot
extrude every one whose absence would make
the nucleus purer, until we come down to the
old woman who said of a community that hunt-
ed out heretics: 'There is only Jamie and me
left, and I'm no so sure about Jamie.'"

I earnestly believe that we best do our share
of purifying the nucleus by purifying ourselves,
and not by expelling our brothers; that we can
prevent wrong better by holding up lofty ideals,
than by separating ourselves disdainfully from
those we condemn; that the Society lives by
the splendor of its ideals, not by the rigidity
of its lines of exclusion; that it will endure in
proportion to the spirituality unfolded in it smem-
bers, and not according to the plaudits or censures

of the world ; that we strengthen it in proportion as we love and pardon, and weaken it as we condemn and ostracise. Thus believe I. I can no other.

———

I may here state, for the information of younger members, how this article came to be written. It had no reference to my honored and much-maligned friend, Mr. C. W. Leadbeater, for, in the first place, he had resigned from the Society nearly a year before, and I was not dealing with resignations but with expulsions, and, in the second, I knew him to be a man of the noblest and purest character, and I was concerned with 'sinners'. But, in the troublous days of 1906, one of our best members had been expelled from the Theosophical Society for saying, among other things, that the Society had "no moral code". I brought the matter before the General Council by an appeal to the President-Founder, and, with his full consent, the expulsion was cancelled and the member re-instated. While this was pending, I was nominated for the Presidency— in January, 1907—and wrote the above article, deliberately using the same phrase that had formed a charge against the expelled member, in order to see if I should be visited with the same penalty, and also in order that all members of the T. S. might know, before they cast their votes, what would be my policy if elected. The phrase has been wrenched from its context and widely used against me, as showing that I considered morality to be a matter of indifference in the T. S. Nothing could be further from the truth. It is as though it were said that the *Bible* declares: "There is no God"—a statement literally true but made to convey a lie. For the sake of the many good people who have been distressed by the false interpretation put upon my words, I have reprinted this article.

The Basis of the T. S. is the recognition of Brotherhood and nothing should be added to this as a condition of admission, nor to its denial as a reason for expulsion. It exists to spread this recognition, and accepts as members those only who desire to help in the spreading. Those only who reject this condition, who deny Brotherhood, should be expelled. And the expulsion is not a penalty for wrong-doing, but the inevitable result of their giving up the object for the promotion of which they entered.

It is my profound conviction that a spiritual Society may not, without committing suicide, drive away the sinner instead of seeking to redeem him; that it cannot have a moral code, enforced by penalty on its members. And this, not merely

15

on the common-sense view enunciated by the
house-holder in the parable of Christ (*S. Matt.* xiii.
28, 29), that in the effort to root out the bad,
the good may also be torn up; but on the far
deeper principle that we are our younger brothers'
keepers; that evil is not destroyed by evil, but
by good; that the Law of Moses may be necessary
for the maintenance of a State, but the Spirit of
the Buḍḍha and the Christ is the very life of a
spiritual Society; that the helping of the weak
is the duty of the strong; that the sinner may
be rescued by the company of the good, but never
by being driven away from them. As the Messenger
of the White Lodge, I must proclaim and strive to
act on its eternal principle, that "Love is the ful-
filling of the Law".

ADYAR,   ANNIE BESANT.
24*th June*, 1910.

NOTES

NOTES

NOTES

NOTES

NOTES

NOTES

NOTES

NOTES

Printed in Great Britain
by Amazon